OF

EAST ANGLIA

Front cover picture: Ipswich, 1921

Above: Market Place, King's Lynn, 1898

FRANCIS FRITH & HIS UNIQUE ARCHIVE

In 1860, Francis Frith, the Quaker son of a Chesterfield cooper, was 38 years old. He had already sold a massive grocery business he had built up, for a small fortune. Like Livingstone and Stanley, Frith was fired with a romantic wanderlust, and the Victorian deep passion for travelling and exploring. Between 1857 and '59 he made several pioneering photographic journeys to remote regions of the Nile that brought him considerable fame.

After his marriage in 1860, he confined his wanderings a little closer to home and began a series of photo trips around Britain. His aim was to make his pictures available to the greatest number of people possible - life was hard and drab for millions of Victorians, and Frith believed his 'view souvenirs' of seaside resorts, beauty spots and town and village scenes would help keep their rare days out alive in their memories. He was right: by 1890 he had created the largest photographic publishing company in the world!

As well as thousands of views of high streets around Britain, Frith's growing archive included beautiful scenes of leafy glades, dusty lanes, rocks and coastlines, and the boats and riversides, beloved of Victorian wanderers like Jerome K Jerome - whose 'Three Men in a Boat' had struck a strong chord with the public.

Life in the Frith family was never dull. The family went with him on many trips, and the highlights were recorded by his wife, Mary Ann, in her journal. In 1872 she tells of a relaxing three week expedition to Ilfracombe in North Devon. Whilst such trips may have been something of a holiday for his wife and children, Francis Frith found no time to put his feet up. He was up and down the coast photographing Barnstaple and Lynton, hiring carters to carry him out to remote locations, and boatmen to row him round the bay to view and photograph spectacular cliff formations.

After Francis Frith died in 1898 his sons carried on the business for many years with great success, specialising in postcards and other prints. So impressive is the archive he started that **The Financial Times** called it '*a unique and priceless record of English life in the last century*'.

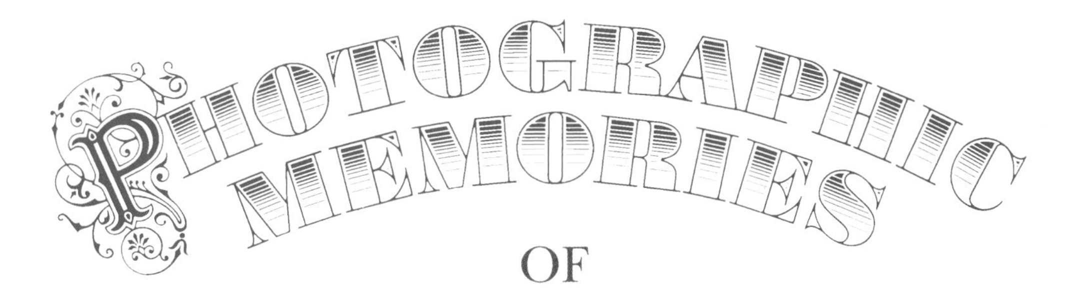

OF

EAST ANGLIA

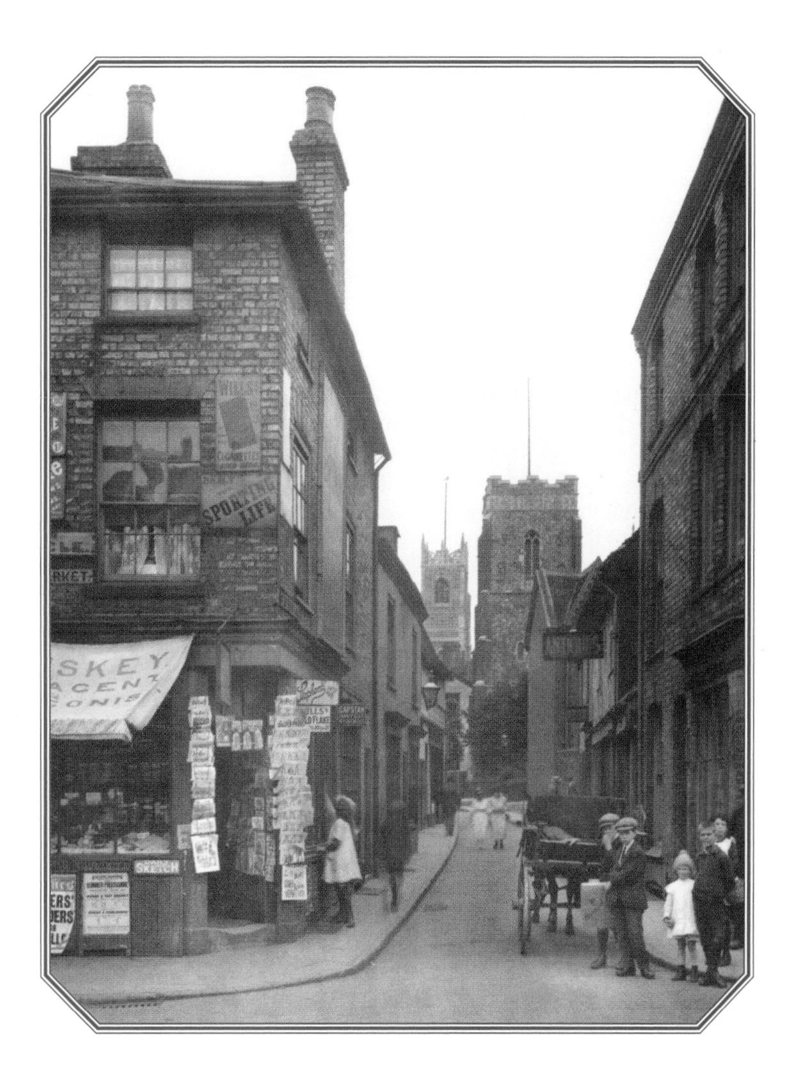

This edition published by
The Francis Frith Collection exclusively for
Selecta Books Ltd., Roundway, Devizes,
Wiltshire SN10 2HR
in association with Michael Brewer.

First published 1995

ISBN 1 85937 016 0

Printed in Singapore

Reproductions of all the photographs in this book are available as framed or mounted prints. Apply to The Francis Frith Collection and quote the title of this book.

The Francis Frith Collection
The Old Rectory, Bimport, Shaftesbury, Dorset SP7 8AT
Tel: 01747 855669 Fax: 01747 855065

Contents

SUDBURY. This fine old wool town, with its busy agricultural market, sits snugly in a loop of the Stour, the beautiful river made famous by John Constable, painter of quintessentially English landscapes. It is also the birthplace of Gainsborough, another famous painter of landscapes and people. Blessed with more than its fair share of fine houses, Sudbury offers visitors a strong sense of history.

Right: North Street, Sudbury in 1895. On the right are two of the town's popular pubs - the Dragon and the White Horse - the latter with an elegant statue over the bay window. They would have been packed with farmers on market days.

Above: The Mill at Sudbury in 1895. A fine old weather-boarded building on the river. **Opposite: Market day at Sudbury in 1904.** The jostling famers gossip and trade. There are harrows, wheelbarrows and horse-drawn grass cutters for sale; on the left a small crowd watches a demonstration - country markets were a favourite place for manufacturers to offer new-fangled inventions and devices. Farmers were eternally sceptical, always wishing their neighbours to waste their money first before they themselves would shell out.

Milliner BOWLES. Draper
XCHANGE

Top: Needham High Street in 1922. This small town has always been busy with traffic. Stage coaches once rattled through on the way to Ipswich and Bury St Edmonds, and later motorcars thundered along the long street, shaking the foundations of its old Georgian buildings. Note the fine wrought-iron hanging sign of the King's Head, enticing travellers to halt and break their journey.

Left: Willy Lott's Cottage at Flatford Mill in 1906. Here Constable, our greatest landscape painter, enjoyed his carefree boyhood: '*The sound of water escaping from mill-dams, willows, old rotten planks...I love such things...those scenes made me a painter, and I am grateful.*'

Previous pages: A busy market scene on Market Hill at Sudbury, in 1904. In the background is the fine Victorian Corn Exchange, where farmers brought their samples of corn to sell to the corn merchants.

Above: Barking Tye in 1934. A shepherd folds his flock.

Above: High Street, Hadleigh in 1922. With its long street of historic inns and fine old buildings - such as the one illustrated here - Hadleigh has long been a favourite haunt of travellers.

IPSWICH. Set on the River Orwell, this bustling port, for centuries Suffolk's county town, traded cloth with the countries of Europe. By the turn of the century many of the town's exquisite timber-framed buildings had already been lost, yet Cobbett, just a few generations earlier, was fulsome in his praise: '*Fine, populous, beautiful, well paved, everything good and solid, no wretched buildings to be seen on its outskirts.*' Praise indeed from a critic notoriously hard to please.

Top: Sailing barge and steamer on the Orwell in 1921. The local mills all owned fleets of sailing barges which plied up and down the river. **Above: The Butter Market, Ipswich in 1893.** This marvellous photograph depicts the town as it must have looked for many centuries, until cars, one-way streets and chainstores altered its character irrevocably. There are horse-drawn carts and wagons and a plethora of small shops, which are displaying as many of their wares as they can outside. Note Webbs' colossal sign at the end of the street. Set against Levi & Co's, it looks like a game of shopkeepers' scrabble. On the right is the famous Ancient House.

Top: St Peter's Dock, Ipswich in 1921. The Industrial Revolution brought much heavy industry to the town, including makers of agricultural machinery like Ransome's, boiler makers and other engineering concerns. In the background are Burton's and Cranfield's, the latter one of the town's massive mills. Goods are being loaded and unloaded onto sailing barges from the railway trucks on the quay. In the background is a steamship - cargoes were often temporarily offloaded from bigger ships onto barges, so that they were light enough to steam through to the Wet Dock, built by the Victorians in the early 1840s.

Left: The Ancient House, Ipswich in 1893. Built in 1567, this is the architectural gem of the town, with elegant oriel windows and decorative pargeting. These plasterwork panels, showing 80 people and animals, represent the continents of the world as they were known at the time.

Top: The Butt and Oyster Inn, Ipswich in 1910. A charming old inn, haunt of sailors, on the breezy banks of the river.
Above: The Docks, Ipswich in 1893. Ropes are coiled neatly on the barge in the foreground. On the right, a sailing ship is being unloaded. **Opposite: Old Cattle Market, Ipswich in 1921.** A captivating step back in time...children stand and stare at the Frith photographer. Hiskey's the newsagent offers comics and advertises the papers of the day - the London Chronicle, The Daily Chronicle and The People. From the headline on the billboard, it looks like the miners are threatening a strike - their leaders are holding a ballot.

WILLS'S
CIGARETTES
SPORTING LIFE
MARKET
HISKEY
SKETCH
MINERS'
LEADERS
FOR
CAPSTAN

ELIXSTOWE. With its shingly south-facing beach set in a broad breezy bay, its half-mile pier, municipal gardens and pavilion, Felixstowe was a favourite holiday destination for the late Victorians and Edwardians. It grew rapidly after the railway arrived in 1877. It was also a prosperous and thriving port, with a sizeable dock and quay linked to Ipswich by rail.

Right: Felixstowe Beach in 1899.
Holidaymakers shelter from the harsh sun under dark umbrellas. Everyone is dressed very formally - the women in starched dresses and blouses, and the men in stiff-necked shirts and suits. Yet what the Victorian holiday resort lacked in colour it made up for in noise and exuberance. Many of these trippers laboured long and hard throughout the year and looked forward with longing to their brief, happy time away from the factories and machine shops. They bought postcards, too - many from Frith & Co - so that they could relive the joyous moments through the long winter months.

Below: The Beach, Felixstowe in 1899.
All aboard for a trip round the bay! You could hire a rowing boat or sailing dinghy. Or, if you were feeling really idle, steamers would carry you up the coast to Yarmouth or to Walton on the Naze.

Top: Out for a ride, Felixstowe, 1907. A very elegant donkey carriage carries a well-to-do lady on a sight-seeing trip round the town. She is well tucked up to keep the sea breezes at bay. Her children have chosen smart little carts pulled by goats.

Left: The Gardens and Cliff Hotel, Felixstowe in 1907. On the right is one of the town's grandest hotels, with wrought-iron balconies and unsurpassed sea views. It was converted to offices during this century. Felixstowe's 20-foot wide promenade was built in 1902, and stretches two miles from the Manor House to Cobbolds Point.

Top: Bawdsey in 1907. Set close by the mouth of the River Deben, this peaceful village was the home of a small lobster fleet, but was better known to travellers for its ferry over to Felixstowe. Many ships were wrecked off the coast here, and the village was infamous as the haunt of smugglers. Here, children play on the broad green. Behind is the Ferry Boat Inn.

Left: Bawdsey in 1907. A charming village scene. Villagers pose for the Frith photographer. They would enjoy considerable fame, appearing on Frith & Co postcards in shops all over the region.

Opposite top: Bawdsey in 1894. Rowing boats rock in the shallows. Others are hauled up onto the shingle.

Opposite below: Walton in 1899. Now an outlying suburb of Felixstowe, Walton once had a charming, dusty village street.

WOODBRIDGE. Once a busy seaport and shipbuilding centre - over 300 ships were registered here in the 17th century - this exquisite little red-brick town is filled to bursting with historic houses and inns. When ships became bigger, they finally outgrew the quays and boatyards of the little port. Now the estuary waters, with their tide mills, marshes, shingle and sandy banks, are the haunt of wading birds, and beloved of artists and naturalists.

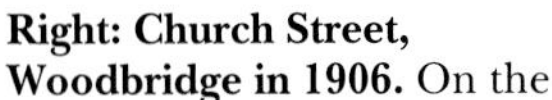

Right: Church Street, Woodbridge in 1906. On the right is one of the town's ancient inns - The Cross - established in 1652. This photograph shows how the rich variety of the town's vernacular buildings, differing considerably in style and proportion, adds charm and dignity to the overall townscape.

Above: The Bell Inn, Woodbridge in 1894. Above this historic inn, with its jettied upper storey, is the old steelyard, which was used for weighing wool, hides and hay. It is the only example left in Suffolk. The landlord stands proudly at the door. Beyond the inn, on the right, is a beautiful little Georgian bay window, in use as a tradesman's workshop.

Above: The Shire Hall, Market Hill, Woodbridge in 1908. Built by the town's great benefactor, Thomas Seckford, this fine 16th century building, with its stone quoins and rich dark brickwork, housed the Corn Exchange and covered market on its ground floor. Farmers' carts could be driven straight through the archway. The Flemish style gables were added in the 17th century. Set all around the square are houses and shops full of character and individuality, contributing to the harmonious and lively street scene.

Left: The Bull Hotel, Woodbridge in 1938. Tennyson stayed in this famous hotel as the guest of the poet Edward Fitzgerald.

Right: Trimley Village, 1899. This charming village street scene of a hundred years ago, with its network of shading trees, would not look as peaceful as this in a modern photograph. Now cars and lorries thunder through bound for Ipswich and Felixstowe. On the left is the Three Mariners Inn.

Below: Middle Hill, Wickham Market in 1929. A street of simple cottages, plainly plastered. It was said that the villagers used to gather at their windows in Wickham Market to watch the carts carrying the wounded of Waterloo from warships on the coast to military hospitals inland.

Top: Market Hill, Wickham Market in 1928. This small town once had a bustling medieval market which filled the broad and spacious square to overflowing. By 1928 the square was little more than a windy carpark. Yet the picture shows the pleasing Georgian brick facades that retain the town's unique charm. **Above: Market Hill, Wickham Market in 1928.** You would never guess that the town once boasted an ironworks that manufactured steamengines and machinery for wind and water mills.

ALDEBURGH. "*Could any town be more pleasant to come to than this, with its quaint sea-fretted beach and three streets in a row?*" This is one of many accolades given to this enchanting little fishing town over the years. Birthplace of the poet Crabbe, and once one of the leading seaports on the east coast, Aldeburgh had a thriving ship-building industry. When the lower reaches of the Alde silted up the town was left stranded, a haven for yachtsmen and visitors.

Right: The Steps, Aldeburgh in 1906.
A steep passage leads down to the sea's edge. Here lived many of the town's fishermen and their families. The yards rang to the cries and laughter of children. As in all fishing communities the fisher families were tightknit and fiercely independent. They could hardly be otherwise - once they were out on the treacherous seas in their 'punts' they had nothing to fall back on other than their own native wit and resourcefulness.

Below: High Street, Aldeburgh in 1909.
By 1909 the town was already a favourite with visitors. Here traps ply for trade and two girls brave the main street on cycles. Much of the town was built up at this time - you can see two brand new matching houses with bay windows on the left.

Top: Slaughden Quay, Aldeburgh in 1906. Much of the town of Aldeburgh that the Elizabethans knew has now disappeared under the sea. Here at Slaughden there were flourishing shipbuilding yards and a hamlet, long since submerged. The loss of shipbuilding brought much suffering to Aldeburgh, reflected in the poet Crabbe's portrait of the town, 'The Borough'.

Left: Aldeburgh in 1929. A lively summer holiday scene in the main street. Children meet their friends in the middle of the road, and Ward's bus has been hired for an excursion.

Top: Moot Hall, Aldeburgh, 1906. This curious old building, also known as the Guild Hall, once stood in the centre of the town of Aldeburgh, but owing to the encroachments of the sea, it was actually standing on the beach by the time this picture was taken. **Below: The Parade, Aldeburgh, 1906.** A panorama of the town's waterfront. In the distance is one of the watchtowers owned by the 'beach companies' that pre-dated the Aldeburgh lifeboat. These salvage companies were quick to put to sea if a potential wreck was spotted. **Opposite: The Harbour, Aldeburgh, 1906.** A tranquil view over the harbour. The little boy posing for the photograph provides a perfect foil for the picturesque collection of somewhat dilapidated boats.

THORPENESS. This pleasant and peaceful little resort is three miles up the coast road from Aldeburgh. It is set on the site of the historic fishing village of Thorpe, and was planned as a seaside resort by Stuart Ogilvie in the early 1900s.

Top: Thorpeness in 1929. Children enjoy a safe afternoon out on the lake in a boat rowed by their older brother.
Above: Thorpeness in 1929. A panoramic sweep of the coast looking back towards Aldeburgh. The many vintage cars would delight a collector today.

Top: The Lake, Thorpeness in 1922. This 65 acre lake, known locally as 'the Mere', was constructed in 1910 as a safe boating centre. Although it was primarily a place for holidays, Thorpeness still had a colony of fishermen who hung their nets to dry outside the old timber church.

Left: Orford Village in 1909. A charming view of Orford's lovely old square. Famous for its imposing Norman castle keep - visible in the background - Orford was once a thriving port with its own fleet of barges and schooners, sending wool and cloth to Europe. This all came to a sad end when the river silted up. By 1909 Orford came to life only in the holiday season. It wasn't just the sea that caused Orford to shrink: it is said that a local doctor once had a whole row of cottages demolished in the town because the inhabitants disturbed him with their noise.

Top: Leiston in 1922. This thriving industrial town sits in the deep countryside bordering the Suffolk coastline. It all began in the 1720s when the local blacksmith, a Mr Garrett, set up a workshop for making agricultural tools. By the end of the Victorian era it had developed into the thriving 'Leiston Works', manufacturing heavy machinery. **Above: High Street, Leiston in 1922.** The once tiny community grew dramatically, and the green and leafy village lanes were lined with spanking new brick houses for the workers.

Top: Leiston Abbey in 1894. Out in the fields beyond the town are the romantic ruins of what once must have been one of the most beautiful of England's abbeys. Its grey walls have been crumbling for centuries and its stone Gothic arches frame the wide blue Suffolk sky. Seven centuries old, it was turned into a farmyard at the Dissolution; then cattle grazed the aisles and nave where once the monks knelt down to pray. Here we see it at its most prosaic: wood is piled in rough heaps and broken gates and rubble walls divide the holy space. Yet it offers a welcome atmosphere of peace and calm in such a busy, industrial locality.

Left: The lane to the Abbey in 1894. The old walls are smothered in ivy, which increases the air of mystery and solitude.

SAXMUNDHAM. This unassuming market and agricultural town straddles the Ipswich to Yarmouth highway, and is crossed by the less frenetic country road between Leiston and Framlingham. With its leafy approach avenues, twisting streets and quiet market square, it has offered travellers over the years a welcome break from the hubbub of the road.

Right: The Bell Hotel, Saxmundham in 1929. This fine old coaching inn was rebuilt in the 1840s. Note its lordly Tuscan-style porch. On the left a chauffeur poses proudly by his master's motor car, one foot on the running board.

Above: High Street, Saxmundham in 1929. This bustling street of small shops includes the Chocolate Box Tea Rooms, recommended by the Cyclists Touring Club; also a branch of the Leiston Industrial Cooperative Society, and Hayward & Sons' heating and water supply engineers. Two small girls wait patiently to cross the road.

Top: The Bell Hotel, Saxmundham, 1929. Saxmundham was always an important coaching town; the Yarmouth Mail called four times a day, thundering through the narrow streets and turning on a sixpence into the Bell Inn yard. Here the hotel is calling itself the 'Headquarters for Motorists, Saxmundham'.

Left: Saxmundham in 1929. One of the town's pleasing leafy avenues. On the right is Waller & Sons, the wine merchants. A horse and cart is unloading crates of beer. Mr Waller was obviously a man keen to make an impression on clients. Look how he has extended his simple cottage premises, which were originally in line with those adjoining. The magnificent Romanesque-style colonnade is impossible to miss.

FRAMLINGHAM. Set on one of Suffolk's low and unspectacular hills, Framlingham is an ancient market town of great character, with fine buildings, a magnificent church and an impressive many-towered castle - one of the most imposing ruins in England. John Evelyn, the diarist, gives the town a curious and unexpected accolade: Framlingham is '*famous for producing the tallest and largest oak trees, perhaps in the world*'.

Opposite top: Framlingham in 1929. Cars park haphazardly in the broad, triangular market square. **Opposite below: Market Hill, Framlingham in 1909.** Note the unusual screen of pollarded trees. It hides A T Wicks' elegant Georgian premises. The blinds are down to shade the sun. Behind is the tower of St Michael's church, with its fine 15th century battlemented tower, almost a hundred feet high. **Top: Market Hill, Framlingham in 1909. Above: Framlingham from Albert Place in 1909.** The tall village pump is on the left.

Right: Dunwich Village in 1909. Called by some 'a dead city', little is left of the great town that Dunwich once was. There were nine churches, and the last, All Saints, crumbled into the sea in 1919, to follow the rest of the town's buildings. Now there is only this quiet village lane with its few cottages. Legend has it that local fishermen, threading their way back through the treacherous seas to a safe haven, still hear the bells of the lost churches.

Below: Yoxford Village in 1909. With its reputation as 'the garden of Suffolk' and its cornucopia of fine buildings and pretty thatched cottages, Yoxford has attracted travellers for generations. Here the dusty main street winds by 'Ye Olde Confectionery Shoppe', where '*cyclists and tourists may find rest and refreshment*'. Beyond, the village baker stands in his doorway.

Top: Blythburgh Church from the meadows in 1895. This magnificent church has been called the most memorable sight on the road to Yarmouth. It rises like a great ship out of the salt marshes, its noble tower reaching high into the broad blue sky. Inside, the great roof is supported by the spreading wings of wooden angels, that are still peppered with shot from bullets fired in the Civil War. On a dark, stormy day this beautiful church, in its isolated setting, offers a stirring and memorable prospect.

Left: Blythburgh Village, 1895. The village, a few miles inland from Southwold, is a jumble of simple, neat cottages and one or two more ornate houses built in the Arts and Crafts era.

Top: Walberwck Village in 1919. Now a peaceful village, beloved of artists, Walberswick was once a busy fishing and shipbuilding community. Here, a travelling fruiterer and vegetable merchant offers visitors fresh local produce from his cart.

Left: Walberswick Bridge in 1919. This ramshackle bridge connects Walberswick village with the coast path to Southwold, across the Blyth estuary. Washing hangs out to dry in the sea breezes at the backs of the cottages.

Opposite above: The Blyth estuary at Walberswick in 1891. The muddy estuary with its tumble down piers and fishermen's huts was a favourite subject of the great painter Phillip Wilson Steer.

Opposite below: The old pontoon chain ferry, Walberswick in 1919. Prone to breaking down and even sinking, this old ferry made the short journey across the Blyth a major adventure.

LT782
GY686

Stephens
AGENT

TOWN HALL
BEWARE of MOTORS
FIRE STATION
SWAN

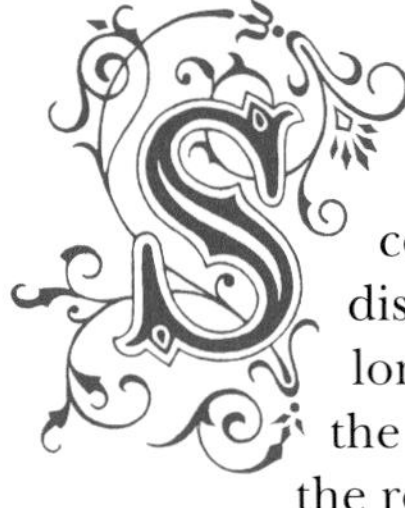

SOUTHWOLD. Set on the low cliffs facing the North Sea, Southwold must be one of the most beautiful small towns in Britain. With its wide greens, its colour-washed cottages with pantiled roofs, and its historic fishing fleet, it offered everything the discerning holiday maker could possibly wish for: comfortable hotels and good shops, a long stretch of beach, and bracing walks over the wide salt flats. At night, a stroll along the front was a stimulating experience, with the lighthouse flashing out its warning over the roof tops and flooding the gable walls with ghostly light.

Previous page: Market Place, Southwold in 1919. On the right is the elegant and famous Swan Hotel.

Right: The Green, Southwold in 1896. The town's seven famous greens were created as a result of the great fire of 1659, which destroyed very many of the town's old buildings.

Above: The Promenade, Southwold in 1893. On the left is the Sailors' Reading Room, where the local fishermen would spend their few hours of leisure discussing the events of the day or enjoying a game of cribbage. Visitors have always been welcome; prints and photographs cover the walls, showing the town's fishermen and their boats. There are also pictures and newspaper clippings showing the rescues made by the local lifeboat crew - they make moving reading.

Top: The Beach, Southwold in 1896. Using the windlasses, fishermen have hauled in their boats onto the shingle. In the background a little steamer sends a black scribble of smoke into the clear sky. Domesday records the town as being a major fishing port, paying 20,000 herrings each year to the Lord of the Manor. Yet in the centuries that followed, a shingle bar gradually blocked the harbour mouth and destroyed the town's prospects of developing into a major east coast port.

Left: On the Beach, Southwold in 1906. Holidays at Southwold were dignified and salubrious affairs. There was fun and jollity, but it was always a little restrained and self-conscious - the town frowned at any suggestion of the indecent or brash.

OWESTOFT is set on the fringes of the Broads, at the eastern extremity of England. With its broad, sandy beaches, its historic port and fishing fleet, Lowestoft has long been a bustling and cosmopolitan seaside town. Its two halves are connected by a swing bridge; the south end of the town is the province of bathers and visitors, the north - with its narrow lanes known as the Scores - the thriving port, industrial and commercial area.

Right: The entrance to the harbour, Lowestoft in 1887. The fishing harbour with its trawlers is at the heart of the town. Great ketch-rigged sailing trawlers plied between Lowestoft and the rich fishing grounds of Dogger Bank. After the railway came, Lowestoft grew even more prosperous; it was now possible for fish to be transported swiftly all over the country. The harbour rang to the cries of the fishermen and their wives, the latter working in the kipper-curing houses. The fishing nets were dried over wooden frames.

Below: The Yacht Basin, Lowestoft in 1896. Here in the outer harbour, alongside the South Pier, the seagoing activities and chat were more leisurely and recreational, with old yacht club salts swapping stories over a pink gin.

Top: The Pier from the Sands, Lowestoft in 1896. A man offering donkey rides stands on the beach. In the background is a forest of masts from the yacht basin. **Above: The South Pier Reading Room, Lowestoft in 1896.** A day out at the seaside could be a very formal affair for the Victorians. The man in the top hat could be bound for a board meeting in the city rather than a stroll in the sunshine.

Right: Lowestoft in 1922. A day to wrap up against the wind, stay dry, and wait patiently for lunch. The clouds are thickening and waves crash against the sea wall drenching with spray the few holidaymakers foolhardy enough to venture too close.

Above: Oulton Broad, Lowestoft in about 1870. One of the most magnificent stretches of inland water in England. Visitors could hire boats of every description, including the beautiful old wherries. Oulton was a paradise for the novice seafarer.

Top: The Convalescent Home, Lowestoft in about 1875. With its healthy sea breezes and clear air, Lowestoft was the perfect place for the sick and ailing to recover their strength and well-being. Here an informal group enjoy an afternoon in the garden, reading, playing croquet or just lounging around in the sun.

Left: London Road, Lowestoft in 1896. By the end of Queen Victoria's reign, the chain stores were competing for the poor man's wages. Their tills chimed merrily until late in the day. Gone was personal service and the guarantee of local produce. What these stores did guarantee were low prices, something the poor man could not ignore easily. Here, Boots the Chemist is blazing its message to the local population. It was opening up similar branches all over the country.

BECCLES. A thousand years ago the waves lapped at the fringes of this market town. Now the sea is several miles away, and the land in between reclaimed and rescued. Set on the south bank of the River Waveney, and highly popular with boating enthusiasts, Beccles is an historic town that has seen much rebuilding, owing to a number of disastrous fires in the 16th and 17th centuries. Yet the town still has many fine buildings to delight visitors.

Right: Dunberry Boathouse, Beccles in 1894. The boatman poses amongst the reeds for the photographer. The boat certainly looks comfortable - it has a quilted seat. Francis Frith very often relied on the local knowledge of boatmen and carters to tell him about picturesque subjects and vistas.

Above: Market Square, Beccles in 1900. It is a sunny day in the town, and too hot for much work to be done. The blinds are down over the shops. Note the great variety of simple, dignified buildings. The ironmonger's huge new sign is masking the upper storey gables. The shopkeeper must be using the upstairs rooms as a storage area. In the background is St Michael's Church.

Top: Market Place, Beccles in 1894. On the left is a fine terrace of Georgian brick buildings with decorative stone dressings around the windows. Note the unusual round chimneys of the 'The People's Clothier', and the Dutch-influenced gables of the house on the extreme left. Decorators are up the ladder painting the windows. **Above: Beccles from the bridge, 1894.** The town was once a flourishing port: all along the river were staiths where corn, coals and malt were hauled by barges and wherries up and down the coast.

Right: Geldeston Lock, near Beccles, 1894. Here visitors idled and picnicked under the willow trees, watching the river craft glide by into the lock.

Below and Opposite: Somerleyton Hall, near Beccles in 1891. The railway contractor, Samuel Peto, bought the old manor of Somerley in the 1840s and immediately remodelled the entire building. The new design is generally considered to be uninspired and coarse. The architect was John Thomas, the sculptor of many of the statues at the Houses of Parliament; there is a lofty Italianate tower, stable block, many cottage ornés - and the conservatory, shown opposite. The effect is magnificent, with slim columns supporting an elegant and spectacular glass dome. Ferns, exotic plants and statuary combine to create an appealing tropical fantasy.

BURY ST EDMUNDS. This historic abbey and market town has a long history - a millenium ago pilgrims came from all over Britain to pray at the shrine of the martyred King Edmund. Here, too, occurred another important event in Engish history - the barons met and resolved to persuade King John, by force if necessary, to seal Magna Carta. With its lovely old streets, fine buildings and spacious market square, Bury St Edmunds has long been a favourite haunt of travellers.

Right: Churchgate, Bury St Edmunds in 1929. The massive Norman bell tower stands as solid as a castle keep, guarding the entrance to the town. It was once the abbey main gate.

Above: Crown Street, Bury St Edmonds, 1929. Here we see the magnificent tower and clerestory of the church of St James, with its fine Victorian nave roof by Gilbert Scott. This historic street winds its way down to the old Theatre Royal, a celebrated Regency building of 1819 - it was created by William Wilkins, the architect of the National Gallery.

Top: Market Place, Bury St Edmunds in 1898. Customers are waiting for the Post Office to open on the left. Further on, the traders are starting to set up. One is selling mesh fencing, and just beyond is a Lipton's sign - this may be the stall of a coffee grinder and tea dealer. **Above: The arch of the great Norman Tower, Bury St Edmunds in 1898.** This monumental building has been called one of the purest examples of Norman architecture in England.. It s walls are six feet thick and it stands 86 feet high.

Newmarket. Straddling one of the oldest thoroughfares in England, Newmarket is the heart of English horse racing. On the downland around the town are many of the most famous studs in the land, and for four hundred years or more the town's streets have echoed to the clatter of hooves.

Top: High Street, Newmarket in 1922. Set on the great road to Norwich, the town is a natural stopping off point for travellers. Here, Crisswells announce their motor depot and garage services on an elegant wrought iron signboard set high up above the roof. **Above: High Street, Newmarket in 1929.** It is market day, and the pavements are jammed to bursting point with stalls and keen shoppers. A policeman stands in the centre of the street to direct traffic. Newmarket is a town of bicycles - everyone seems to be riding one.

Top: The Grand Stand, Newmarket in 1922. This famous course is out on the heathland at the entrance to the town. The first recorded race was held here in 1619. Macaulay reported that half the dukes in England could be found in and around the stand. Horses are not only raced at Newmarket, they are bought and sold. At the December sales, earlier this century, over 1000 horses transferred ownership.

Left: Horses on the gallops, Newmarket, 1922. Out on the gallops, to the north-west of the town, stable lads put hundreds of throughbreds through their paces in the early morning mists. The scene is noisy and breathtaking, with the thundering of hooves over the grass slopes.

Top: High Street, Mildenhall in 1925. Set alongside the River Lark, this pleasing little brick town has the largest parish in the county, half of which is mere and fen. Here we see some of its fine old shop fronts, with their mullioned windows and decorative facias. Note the old-style awning on the left, held up by wooden poles in the gutter. The animal foodstuff dealer on the right is bold in his claims - an abundance of hen's eggs is guaranteed by a simple diet of Ovum, Thorley's Poultry Spice.

Left: West Street, Mildenhall, 1925. A leafy avenue of carefully clipped and pollarded trees.

Opposite top: High Street, Mildenhall, 1925.

Opposite below: Mill Street, Mildenhall in 1925.

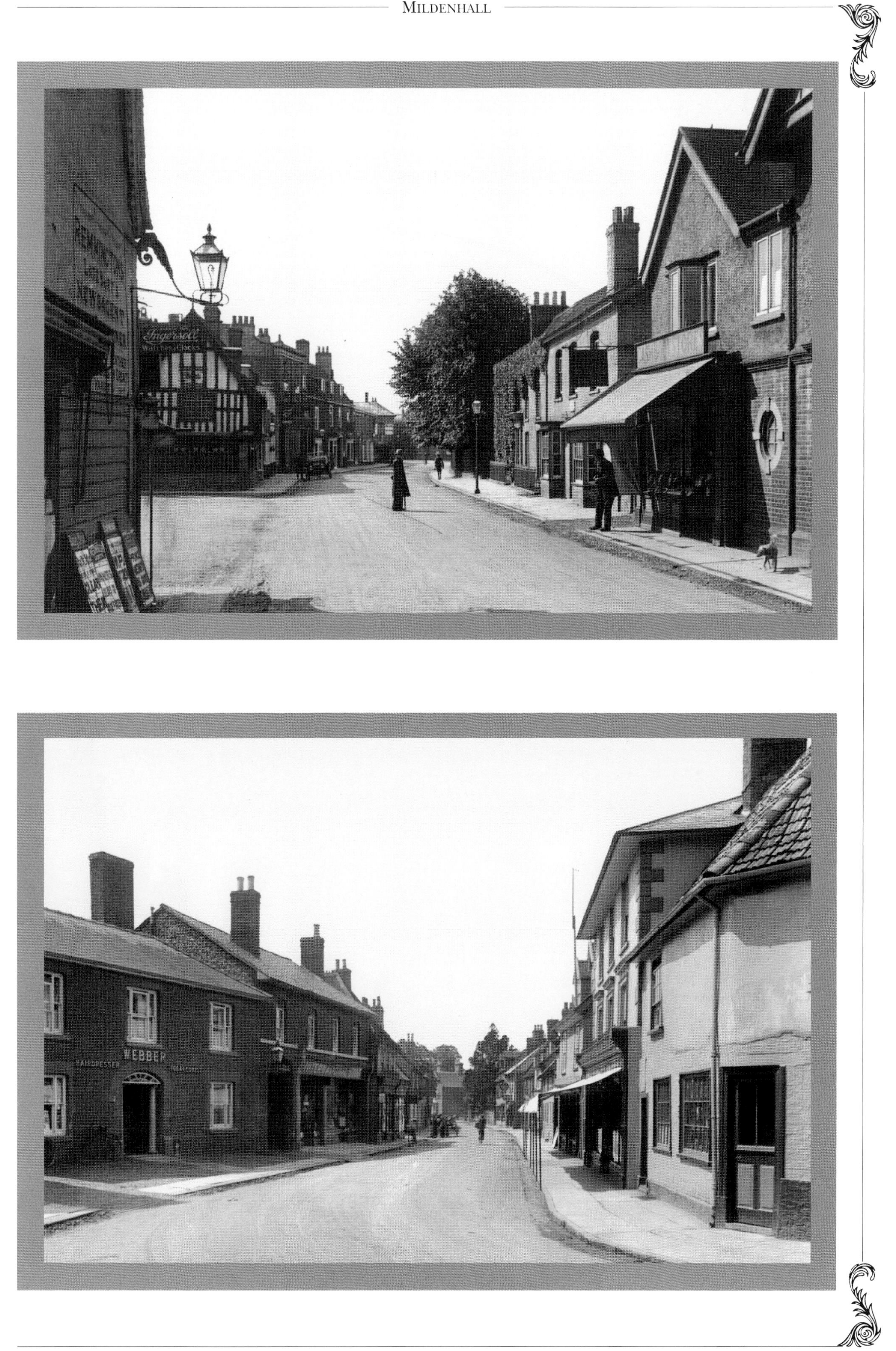
REMMINGTONS
LATE BURT'S
NEWSAGENT
Ingersoll
Watches & Clocks
WEBBER
HAIRDRESSER
TOBACCONIST

RANDON. Situated on the Little Ouse in Breckland country, and on the border with Norfolk, this attractive market town has a long association with the ancient art of flint-knapping. There are flints everywhere - in the surface of the road, set into the walls of houses and in the structure of the church. Knappers are still tapping away at rough pieces of rock in yards in the town, flaking away flint chippings for use as gun flints or for decorative work in building.

Right: Brandon in 1925. At the top end of the broad town street is the Gothic-style school. Built in 1878 by John Lee, it features an imposing clock tower and fine bay windows.On the left is the Five Bells Inn. Note the splendid gilt Hovis sign over the small shop on the corner.

Above: Brandon in 1925. The town displays a harmonious use of local building materials - pantiles, flint, brick, chalk and plaster.

Top: The River Ouse at Brandon in 1925. Once barges navigated the Ouse through the little town on the way to Kings Lynn. Brandon used to be the port for Thetford. An old stone five-arched bridge crosses the river here, linking Suffolk with Norfolk - the Frith photographer is standing at one end taking this picture. Here we have a riverside scene of perfect peace. Punts are moored alongside the old house - including the Nancy Lee. There are rustic chairs and tables on the grass where visitors could sit and enjoy a glass of lemonade and a slab of fruit cake. The reflections penetrate deep down into the silent water.

Left: Brandon in 1925. The pollarded trees bring the town's streets beauty and freshness. The same cannot be said for the telegraph poles further down.

ORWICH. Seventeen roads bring travellers to this great cathedral city. At its heart is the massive Norman castle, surrounded by the old cattle market. Cradled by the waters of the River Wensum, Norwich has its roots deep in the past - from medieval times it was a major wool centre, its textile industry burgeoning further at the end of the 16th century when Flemish and Dutch weavers settled in the city.

Right: Elm Hill, Norwich in 1929. This celebrated cobbled street shows rich medieval plaster and timberwork, with overhanging storeys, gables and dormers. St Peter's Church, at the top, was painted by Cotman, East Anglia's finest landscape painter.

Above: Post Office and Prince of Wales Road, Norwich in 1896. The Royal Hotel on the left is a typical Victorian Gothic creation - heavy and sepulchral. In great contrast, the rich classical frontage of the Post Office opposite offers passers-by a harmonious and airy prospect. In the foreground a young family crosses the road, the children swathed in sparkling white cotton dresses and bonnets. **Opposite: Davey Place, Norwich in 1922.** Empty champagne boxes are stacked outside Bonner's Stores.

OOTS
AND
IOES.
BONSER'S STORES
& COFFEE
MERCHANTS.
BONSER'S STORES
TEAS.
Gilbey's

Top: Pull's Ferry, Norwich, 1891. This tiny canal, with its 15th century gateway, led to the cathedral, and was the route by which the white Caen stone, used to construct the exterior, was carried direct to the masons. The cathedral spire gleams majestically in the distance.

Left: Old Cow Tower, Norwich, 1891. This is down by the river, close by the Bishops' Bridge.

Opposite top: Norwich Market in 1891. St Peter Mancroft rises behind.

Opposite below: Tombland Fair and Castle, Norwich, 1891. '*There is a grey old castle on top of that mighty mound...*' So said George Borrow of this colossal Norman edifice, which acted as the county gaol for centuries. Here at Castle Ditches, drovers urged their beasts to the Saturday markets. In this picture, the hurdled stalls are packed tight with sheep.

Overleaf: Norwich Market Place in 1929.

ISS. This enchanting small town close by the Suffolk border has grown up around a great sheet of placid water - the Diss Mere - which covers six acres. With its many fine old houses and shops, the town has retained its medieval street plan.

Top: Mount Street, Diss in 1925. A pleasing street of jettied houses and simple cottages.
Above: Market Place, Diss in 1925. The town's Friday market was held in this broad space half way up the hill. Rich in Georgian shops with unspoiled frontages, the market place is dominated by the commanding flint-built church of St Mary the Virgin. Its chancel is considered one of the finest examples of knapped flintwork in Norfolk.

Top: Mere Street, Diss in 1925. This broad street narrows sharply as it winds up the hill towards the market place. On the left is West's Garage offering BP car batteries. On sheep or cattle market days this narrow thoroughfare was choked with country folk and farmers.

Left: St Nicholas Street, Diss in 1925. On the left is The Two Brewers Inn and in the distance Garnham's Cash Boot Stores.

HETFORD. At the southern tip of Breckland, this historic market town is graced with many fascinating and splendid buildings of the Georgian era. Almost entirely surrounded by forest and heathland, it was once the capital of Breckland. Ancient earthworks rise up close by the town, reminding us of the dark ages of history that were seen in this wild heathland region, beloved of the writer George Borrow and Norfolk's most illustrious painter, John Crome.

Right: St Peter's Church, Thetford, 1921. The noble tower with its fine flintwork, rebuilt in 1789, casts a deep shadow on the narrow street below. Men stand and gossip, out of the heat of the sun.

Below: Market Place, Thetford in 1929. In the background is the Red Lion Inn.

Above: St Cuthbert's Church, Thetford in 1921. On the right is the Post Office, with characteristic Victorian decorative styling. It looks as if it is market day. A stall is being pushed round the corner on the left and the town's elders are assembling on the corner ready to spot a bargain and mull over the questions of the day. In 1851 the old tower of St Cuthbert's finally collapsed. The church we see here is an almost entirely new creation. Yet the churchwardens are already allowing ivy to invade - it would never be allowed to happen today.

Left: The Grammar School, Thetford in 1921. One of the very oldest in England, Thetford's grammar school was in existence long before the Normans came. The building we see here was constructed in 1876. Tom Paine, renegade, reformer and author of 'The Rights of Man' was taught here.

EAST DEREHAM. With its engineering works and foundry, East Dereham has grown into much more than just a market and agricultural town. Set on the flank of a hill, it gives off a solid, well-built atmosphere, with many pleasing Georgian houses. George Borrow, the 'gypsy scholar,' was born here, and he describes it thus: '*Thou pattern of an English market town, with thy clean but narrow streets branching out from thy modest market place, with thine old-fashioned houses, with here and there a roof of venerable thatch...*'

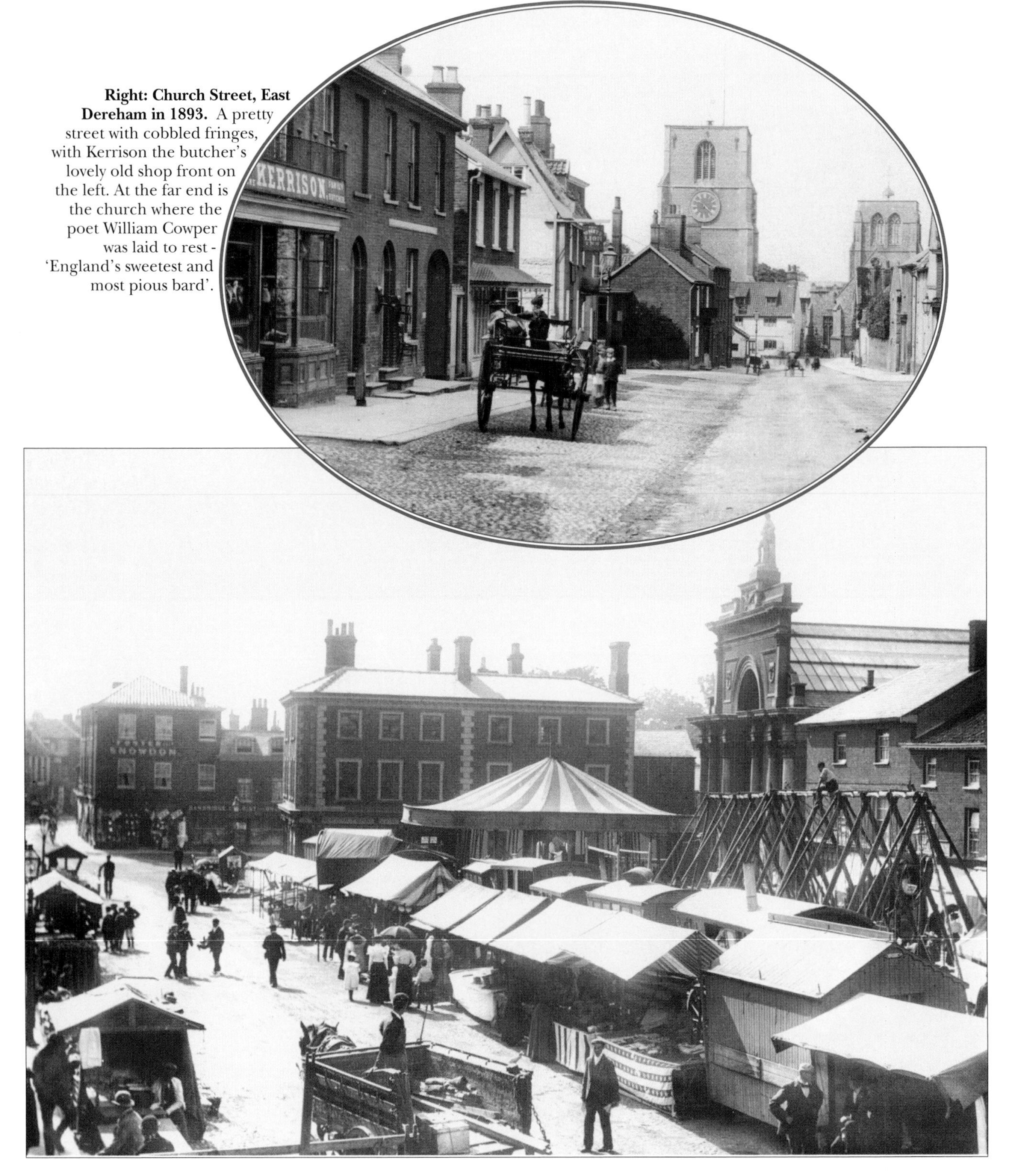

Right: Church Street, East Dereham in 1893. A pretty street with cobbled fringes, with Kerrison the butcher's lovely old shop front on the left. At the far end is the church where the poet William Cowper was laid to rest - 'England's sweetest and most pious bard'.

Above: The Fair, East Dereham in 1898. Although a modest affair in the eyes of city dwellers, this country fair was an important festival day, coinciding with livestock sales and hiring fairs. Brash and gaudy, it was sneered at by the local Temperance group. Yet the steam gallopers with their flaring nostrils, the blaring organ, the stalls offering cheap china, cardboard trumpets and brandy snaps, brought an irresistible glitter and excitement to the quiet country life.

Above: Market Place, East Dereham in 1901. Since first light, drovers have been whipping their cattle along the lanes towards the town. Boys are already hanging around hoping to make a penny or two helping out at the livestock sale. Old houses surround the broad square. With their steep pantiled roofs, odd dormers and gables, and their rich variety of many-paned shop fronts, they show the English market town at its very best.

Left: East Dereham in 1922. A fine vista of the broad market place. You can see how the Victorians adapted older buildings for their own purposes - just beyond the King's Arms Hotel a simple, dignified Georgian house has been given a fashionable rusticated frontage - it was probably carried out by a bank, keen to impress its clients.

Top: Swaffham, 1891. This handsome red-brick market town has a Palladian-style Market Cross. Around the broad market square, where five main roads meet, are some fine Queen Anne and Georgian houses. The magnificent church of St Peter and St Paul has a splendid hammerbeam roof. **Below: Bailey Street, Castle Acre, 1891.** The village street of this hill-top village, on the ancient Peddar Way, is spanned by this imposing towered archway - part of the remains of the old ruined castle, now little more than overgrown fragments of masonry.

KING'S LYNN has been called the most romantic town in England. Its treasurehouse of historic buildings reflects its prosperity down the ages as a flourishing port exporting corn, and importing wine and coal. The River Ouse flows alongside lofty medieval warehouses and staiths, and in the town's narrow streets are many of the fine houses of the merchants who enjoyed the bounty of the town's commercial success.

Top: Norfolk Street, King's Lynn, 1891. A twisting narrow street of old stone setts, gas lamps, Georgian houses with old shopfronts...this view depicts the very essence of the magic of King's Lynn. **Above: Market Place, King's Lynn in 1891.** The traditional market hustle and bustle, with fruit and vegetables and a wide variety of other goods displayed on simple tables under striped awnings and tilts. The whole affair is watched over with a quiet dignity by the town's grand and imposing civic buildings.

LEADER

Top: High Street, King's Lynn in 1908. This fascinating town scene is dominated by Jermyn and Perry's spectacular window display. Victorian shopkeepers enjoyed the luxury of a huge staff - they would have needed a whole brigade of window-dressers to create this visual feast of millinery and fabrics. Some lads loiter on the pavement outside; one is pushing his baby sister around in the simplest pram possible - an orange box fixed to a pair of old wheels. The poor needed to be relentlessly resourceful.

Left: The Customs House, King's Lynn in 1898. Set at the end of King Street, this exquisiite building began its life as the Merchants' Exchange. It was built in 1683. Like so many of the town's buildings, it incorporates lavish amounts of stone - made possible in this stoneless fenland country by the Rivers Nene and the Great Ouse, along which laden barges could navigate.

Opposite: Southgate, King's Lynn, 1891. The traditional entrance into the town from the south, and one of the few remaining features of the town's 16th century walls.

Overleaf: High Street, King's Lynn, 1908. Another street of small, distinctive shops.

CASH & Co
82

Top: Castle Rising in 1898. Once an important port and market centre, the village of Castle Rising has now been forsaken by the sea. Set inside a giant earthwork, its ancient and massive ruinous Norman castle still dominates the landscape. To the right are the remains of the gatehouse and bridge. **Below: Entrance Lodge, Sandringham House, 1896.** Somewhere deep inside this triumph of clipped foliage is the tiny gatehouse to Queen Victoria's renowned royal estate. Even the porch is a hollowed-out close-snipped hedge.

HUNSTANTON was once little more than a peaceful village of creepered cottages, with a disused lighthouse and ruined chapel. Then the railway arrived, and there was such a spate of building that the town grew almost overnight into a prosperous and thriving resort. With its safe, sandy beach, cliff-top walks and comfortable hotels, Hunstanton quickly became a favourite with the Victorian holidaymaker.

Right: The Pier, Hunstanton in 1901. It is early morning. Most of the town's visitors are still at breakfast. It is time for a peaceful perusal of the papers before the crowds arrive, and maybe a gentle stroll along the pier to savour the salt breezes.

Above: The Pier, Hunstanton in 1901. The Victorian advertiser was as keen as his modern counterpart to shout his message abroad. Here the side of the pier proved irresistible. Cash & Co offer 'houses and boots'(!), the King's Lynn & County Stores will deliver your every need direct to your door, and Trenowath Brothers will fill your house with bargain antique furniture.

Top: Hunstanton in 1907. Children enjoy a game of cricket. In the background is the Great Eastern Railway Company Hotel, where the well-heeled would stay. These happy holidaymakers were avoiding many of the sharp east winds that oppressed Norfolk's other resort towns - Hunstanton enjoyed the unique situation of facing west across the Wash, which made it sheltered and balmy.

Left: High Street, Hunstanton in 1907. On the left is Preston's Library, where you could borrow a novel or two to while away the hours. A little further along is one of the town's many private hotels, where less pecunious visitors could stay. There were no balconies and no sea views, but to many people it must have seemed like paradise, compared to life at home in a gloomy back to back terraced house.

Top: Well-next-the-Sea in 1929. Situated on a broad creek, about a mile from the sea, this historic small town has an impressive waterfront, with spacious 18th and 19th century warehouses. It was developed by the Great Eastern Railway - you can see their goods wagons on the quayside.

Left: High Street, Wells in 1929. Its narrow streets cluster around the church. The town has a rich legacy of flint building - see the wall on the left - but many of its fine old buildings have been pulled down over the years and replaced by characterless infill.

Opposite top: The Quayside, Wells, 1929. The Wells whelkers were locally famous, dropping their pots miles out to sea. Being a whelker was not always easy - you could be stranded for hours in bad weather on the wrong side of the harbour, waiting for the tides to cover the bar so that you could get back in.

Opposite below: Esat End, Wells in 1929.

ALSINGHAM has been an important place of pilgrimage since its famous shrine to Our Lady of Walsingham was founded in Edward the Confessor's time. So celebrated was the shrine that it came to be known as 'England's Nazareth'. Surrounded with verdant woods and with a ruined priory and medieval church, Walsingham still exerts a solemn and deeply religious influence on visitors.

Top: The Old Pump, Walsingham in 1922. This worn and weathered medieval pump house is shaped like a huge beehive. With its carved stone dressings, it brings to us a deep sense of the past. Note the brazier on the top.
Above: Sheep going to Walsingham Market, 1929. Shepherds lived solitary lives. Going to market was the time to catch up on gossip, and this shepherd has probably already been chatting with his friends over a glass of ale in the White Hart - you can see it in the background. He doubtless paid a village lad to watch over his flock for a few minutes. The sheep have just been sheared. The sheepdog waits patiently in the foreground, as his old master shufffles on towards Walsingham town.

Top: Market Place, Walsingham in 1922. The Market Place is charming, with many splendid buildings of the 16th century and later, forming a harmonious and very pleasing prospect. On the far left is the old Black Lion Inn.

Left: Old Houses, Walsingham, 1929. With their steep, toppling pantiled roofs, half-timbered walls and jettied storeys, Walsingham's imposing old buildings summon up visions of the holy pilgrimages to the shrine of Our Lady.

Right: Fakenham in 1921. This busy market town nestles on the north bank of the River Wensum. With its cobbled square, fine brick Georgian buildings, red-tiled roofs, and old inn - The Crown - it has been known to travellers for many centuries; it was once a coaching stop, and now attracts visitors on their way to Cromer, Wells and King's Lynn.

Below: Oak Street, Fakenham in 1929.

Top: Melton Constable, 1922. Children play in the dusty road outside a simple street of humble terraced houses. However, Melton Constable is renowned for a very different style of building - its Wren-style country mansion, built in 1670 by Sir Jacob Astley.

Left: Holt Hall, 1896. A picturesque vista of this ancient hall, with its towering chimneys and many gables, cradled in magnificent parkland with noble trees.

Top: Blakeney in 1925. Until the sands silted up its harbour, Blakeney was a flourishing port. Now it sits peacefully amongst the salt marshes, the home of wading birds and yachtsmen. Small boats cluster under the quayside, waiting to sail with the tide. In the background is the sumptuous Blakeney Hotel.

Left: Blakeney in 1925. In the background are the old warehouses that remind us of Blakeney's glorious commercial past. The huge hotel dominates the waterfront.

Opposite top: Blakeney in 1925. Called by many the loveliest village in Norfolk, Blakeney's narrow twisting streets are packed tight with brick and flint cottages.

Opposite below:Cley-next-the-Sea, 1933. A picturesque scene in this old port. The lovely old windmill, dating from 1713, stands on the fringes of the marshes, guarding the town.

SHIP

SHERINGHAM. This hugely popular seaside town grew up in Victorian times around a tiny fishing village. The old cottages cling to the steep cliffs overlooking the sea. All around, new hotels and boarding houses sprang up to cater for the ever-increasing numbers of trippers. The Victorians - great 'fossickers' - were greatly excited by some of the fascinating fossils of animals that were dug out of the town's steep slopes over the centuries.

Previous page: Fishermen at Sheringham in 1893. There is a fierce independence and pride in the expressions and postures of these fishermen. They ventured out into the North Sea in open boats in all weathers.

Right: Sheringham Crabbers in 1906. There was intense rivalry between the Sheringham and Cromer crabbers. They were always raring for a fight or trying to cut each others' ropes.

Above: The Promenade, Sheringham in 1906. Three elegant ladies in white are escorted by a gentleman in an easy stroll along the promenade. Just beyond the breakwater you can just see a line of bell tents on the beach. Behind, rising up the steep hill, are the old cottages of Sheringham, many given over to a new life as lodging houses for visitors.

Top: The Sands, Sheringham in 1921. The perfect English holiday - digging in the soft, squelchy sand, sailing a toy yacht in the shallows or just dawdling about with no particular end in view. Below the sea wall is a line of tottering beach huts. Let's hope they were roped securely down whenever a storm was forecast. In the extreme distance, high up on the cliffs, you can see the highly popular three-mile scenic path to Cromer.

Left: Sheringham fishermen in 1906. These crabbers and lobster fishermen are well covered up against the North Sea storms. They wear the local 'ganseys', thigh length leather sea boots, sou'westers and oilskin jerkins.

Top: East Runton in 1933. We are looking east towards Cromer, which is only a mile or two distant. It is hard to imagine, yet here at East Runton, glaciers smothered the cliffs during the great Ice Age and dumped huge fragments of rock from the Midlands into the sea below. Some ponies are waiting for riders on the sands. The untidy trail of beach huts is a typical feature of the English holiday scene. **Above: West Runton, 1925.** A peaceful scene on the village green, with the local ducks enjoying the sunshine.

ROMER. Like Sheringham, Cromer was once little more than the haunt of crabbers and lobster fishermen, who lived in a jumble of cottages set around the church, with its lofty 160-foot tower. Then the railway came, and the town boomed. Along the seafront a spate of Edwardian hotels soon crowned the clifftops. Now, with its fine beach, crab salads and homely atmosphere, Cromer is justifiably one of the great seaside towns of this exposed and sometimes bleak coast.

Right: Garden Street, Cromer in 1894. A quiet residential street of Edwardian houses. On the right is Mortimers fabric and interiors shop, offering plain and fancy dress materials and rolls of linoleum.

Above: Cromer from the sands, 1899. The church tower rises majestically over the small town. It once served as the town's lighthouse. The bathing machines have been towed down into the shallows. From each one a timid Victorian lady would venture out into the swirling waters. **Overleaf: The Cromer lifeboat, the 'Louisa Heartwell', in 1922.** The tales of the daring rescues made by this famous lifeboat are legion. Its coxwain, Henry Blogg, was the most decorated lifeboatman in Britain, earning three gold and four silver medals, the George Cross and the British Empire medal for his courage. During his 53 years on the Cromer boat 873 lives were saved!

LOUISA HEART

Opposite top: The pier at Cromer in 1902. A young lady stands with her grandmother enjoying the sun and sea breezes - note the heavy, dark clothing of the older woman.The two symbolise the great differences in fashion and outlook between the Victorians and Edwardians.

Opposite below: Cromer, 1906. This views shows the pier and the cliff-top walk. Smart new wooden steps lead down onto the sands.

Right: High Street, Cromer, 1922 A quanint, winding and rather picturesque street which belies its name.

Below: Church Street, Cromer, 1902 Note the sign for Jarrold & Sons over the shop window on the left - one of the old Norfolk families, which is still maintains a major printing business today..

Top: The Post Office, Overstrand in 1921. Two miles from Cromer, this tiny village offered holidaymakers safe, clean beaches and shallow seas - perfect for the great British family holiday.

Left: Overstrand in 1906. A quiet backwater, away from the cries of children and the relentless beating of the waves. A small girl carrying a basket poses with her younger sister.

Right: The Sands at Overstrand in 1906. It may look peaceful enough, yet the coast in these parts has always been in constant danger of coastal erosion, the seas biting into the soft cliffs and carrying away fields and buildings alike - several churches have been washed into the sea. At Overstrand there were originally two churches - one lost its roof in a storm in Victorian times and the villagers thought it prudent to build another alongside. Young men dawdle on the beach in their smart boaters and blazers.

Below: Overstrand in 1906. A cowman drives his ambling dairy herd to the milking parlour through the back lanes of the village. The vast many-chimneyed structure is the prestigious Overstrand Hotel.

Top: The beach, Mundesley on Sea in 1892. A wonderful panorama of the Victorians on holiday. Some of the buildings on the cliff look perilously close to the edge - they could easily collapse and tumble down into the waters below.

Left: Brooke Cottage, Mundesley on Sea in 1921. The poet William Cowper visited this pleasing little seaside resort many times.It is perched high on the windy cliffs. Solid and respectable, and with an expansive beach offering safe bathing, Mundesley was a favourite seaside resort of the Edwardians. A family with their new baby in a pram stroll in the silent lanes away from the sea. In the background you can see the wind-swept cliff-top trees.

Opposite: High Street, Mundesley on Sea in 1921. The old village street, unhurried and timeless. On the left is Dando's general store.

DANDO
K
BOOTS

HORNING. This picturesque village on the banks of the River Bure is in the heart of the Broads. These extraordinary ancient peat-diggings have have found a new lease of life as the most popular inland waterways in the country. Horning, with its ferry, thatched boat-houses and sumptuous riverside lawns, has been a fashionable centre for discerning yachtsmen down the years.

Top: Horning village in 1921. A delightful village scene of pantiles, thatch and eyebrowed dormers.
Below: Horning village in 1934. Two village policemen patrol the village street. Is something amiss? At the Horning branch of Roy's of Wroxham - 'the biggest village store in the world' - customers can buy postcards by one of Frith & Co's major rivals, Raphael Tuck. Note the splendid rustic porch of gnarled and twisted branches on the cottage next door.

Top: Horning village in 1934.

Left: Market Place, North Walsham in 1921. Set between the rivers Ant and Bure, North Walsham was once a famous wool weaving town. Its famous market cross, built in 1550 by Bishop Thirlby, has been restored and repaired many times. On the right, a farmer's two children wait on the wagon whilst their father sells some rabbits to Sewell the butcher. Deep shadows cast a welcome shade across the street. At the town's Paston Grammar School, England's most famous sailor spent three important years of his boyhood - Nelson came here at ten and left in his early teens to go to sea.

PALMERS
WATERSON'S
MOTOR GARAGE
EPPS'S
COCOA
HARRISON'S

GREAT YARMOUTH. Here, three rivers - the Bure, Waveney and Yare - join and flow together into the sea. The town has been a famous port since the times of the Normans, and its herring fleet renowned the world over. With its miles of golden sand, and its position on the fringes of the Broads, Great Yarmouth was quickly discovered by the Victorians, growing rapidly into the major resort town of East Anglia.

Previous page: The Market, Great Yarmouth in 1908. Occupying the entire market place, one of the biggest in England, this giant commercial bonanza stretches as far as the eye can see. On the left is an open-topped tram taking trippers on a sighte-seeing tour.

Right: The Winter Gardens, Great Yarmouth in 1908. A few keen holidaymakers have turned up early to reserve the best seats for the concert at the bandstand.

Above: King Street, Great Yarmouth in 1896. This major shopping street leads out of the market place down towards the river. The shops are busy with deliveries: an assistant on the left is unpacking a wooden crate, and on the right a shop lad waits by a trader's trap outside St George's Hall, the china and glass emporium. There are horses everywhere, the clatter of hooves echoing sharply off the shop facades. Two small boys with impossibly clean collars follow their sister in boater and pinafore - all on best behaviour.

Top: The fishing fleet on the Yare, Great Yarmouth, 1896. Throughout England's history, Great Yarmouth has come to mean herrings. Its great fleet of fishing boats, the numbers swelled each year by 'Zulus' from the north, set out to follow the North Sea herring shoals. It must have been a stirring sight when these graceful boats hoisted their sails and in unison slid out of the harbour into the open sea. The sailing boats were followed in later years by steam drifters. In 1913 the fleet was a thousand vessels strong. In a good season five hundred million herring were netted.

Left: Great Yarmouth, 1887. A panoramic vista of the roofs and chimneys of the town from across the river. Boats rock gently on their moorings.

Top: King's Street, Yarmouth in 1896. A sweltering day in high summer. On the right a shopkeeper is setting up his awning. Decorators have clambered up two pencil-thin, high ladders to paint the top windows of a building on the left. On the right is Johnson the grocer's small handcart. Handcarts were a common sight in Victorian towns. Every trader had a lad who plied the streets making house deliveries. Personal service was a priority to the Victorian shopkeeper.

Left: The Beach, Great Yarmouth, 1887. Pleasure boats are lined up waiting for customers. There is a handy soft drinks stall behind.

Opposite top: The Pier, Great Yarmouth, 1904. Maginficent and imposing, the Britannia Pier was the mecca of entertainment in the town.

Opposite below: The Town Hall, Yarmouth, 1891. This grand Victorian building is typically heavy and Gothic, and replaced a much more graceful Georgian building.

BRITANNIA
PIER

GORLESTON is connected to Yarmouth by a ferry across the Yare. Like its great neighbour, it grew up in the 19th century. With its enchanting old streets, long sandy beach, splendid pavilion and impressive cliffs, it had much to offer those looking for a somewhat quieter life than they might find across the river at Yarmouth. It is said that Gorleston men have the reputation locally of being extremely 'thrifty'. Judging from the town's popularity with visitors, this thrift did not extend to the townsmen's sense of hospitality.

Above: The Sands, Gorleston in 1922. You can see from the fringe of buildings on the cliff that Gorleston is an almost entirely Victorian creation, with custom-built steps, promenade, hotels and lodging houses.

Left: The White Lion Hotel, Gorleston, 1922. Holidaymakers trudge their way back to the hotel after a hard day relaxing on the beach. Note the pleasing terraced houses with fine sash windows.

Opposite top: The harbour at Gorleston, 1894. The fishing fleet sets sail. Steam ships, not dependent on the vagaries of the breeze, lead the way.

Opposite below: High Street, Gorleston in 1908. Like Yarmouth, Gorleston had its own tramway. On the right a hotel has sprung up and cashed in by calling itself 'The Tramway Hotel'.

Index